SCIENCE MADE EASY

Can animals and plants tell the time?

Animals and plants do not know about time. They react to changes in light and temperature. Flowers close their petals at night and some animals hibernate in winter.

What are high and low sounds?

The double bass makes a low sound.

Sounds are vibrations that travel through the air. Because the vibrations travel at different speeds we can tell one sound from another.

Fast vibrations produce a high sound while slow vibrations make a low sound.

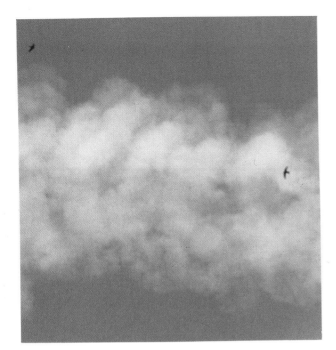

Air is all around us.

What is air?

Air is everywhere. It is made up of different gases, such as oxygen, nitrogen, hydrogen and carbon dioxide. Plants, animals and humans need these gases in order

to live.
Air also contains tiny particles of dust, and in built up areas the air often contains harmful gases from cars and factories.

Why do some things float on water?

Objects float in water if they are less dense and lighter than the amount of water that they have displaced.
A small, solid object, such as a marble, will sink, while a heavy boat, such as a tanker, that displaces more water than its own weight, will float.

It is easy to float on water.

What is a lever?

A lever has an arm which can rock, or pivot, around a support called a fulcrum.
A fulcrum can be anywhere along the length of the arm. Levers are used to move or lift awkward or heavy

The lever moves the points on a track.

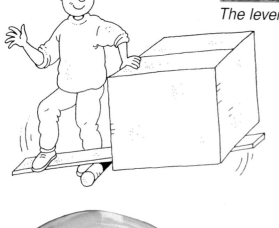

objects. A spade is a type of lever. The handle end is pushed down a longer distance than the other end moves up. This makes it easy to lift a heavy clump of soil.

Why do light bulbs have numbers?

A light bulb is made of glass.

If you look closely at a light bulb, you will see that it has 60W or 100W written on it. The 'W' stands for 'watt'.

A watt is a measurement of electricity that the bulb will use. A 100W bulb will shine brighter than a 60W.

What is water?

As far as scientists know, Earth is the only planet where there is water. Water is created when oxygen and hydrogen molecules combine in a certain way. They join together so that there is 1 oxygen molecule for every 2 hydrogen molecules. That is why you may see water written as H_2O. When water is heated, it evaporates and rises into the air as steam. When water is frozen it becomes solid (ice).

Snow is made of ice crystals.

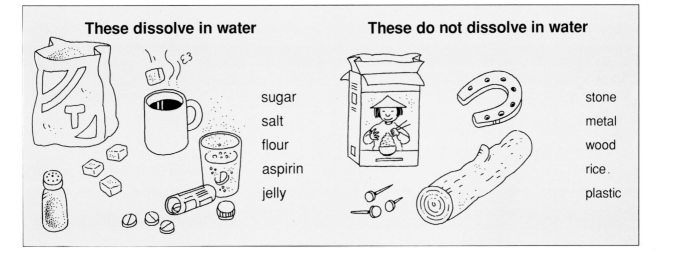

These dissolve in water

sugar
salt
flour
aspirin
jelly

These do not dissolve in water

stone
metal
wood
rice.
plastic

Why do people wear sunglasses?

The ultraviolet rays from the Sun are harmful to skin and eyes. Many of the rays are prevented from reaching us by the ozone layer, but sunglasses protect people's eyes from those that do.

How does sound travel?

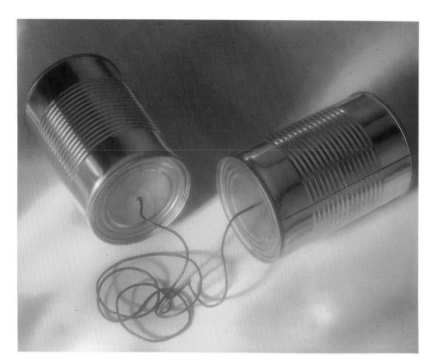

Sounds are vibrations that travel on air waves. When the vibrations hit your ear drum you hear a sound.
If you talk into a tin can that is connected to another can by string, the vibrations travel along the string rather than on air waves. This means that the person talking into one can is able to be heard by the other person who may be standing some distance away.

Sound waves travel along the string of a tin telephone.

Where does daylight come from?

Daylight comes from the Sun. When the Sun sets, the sky becomes dark. However, it can still be quite light at night when there are no clouds and the Moon is full. The Moon itself does not give out light, it reflects light from the Sun.

Darkness falls at sunset.

Why do candles burn?

Candles are made of string surrounded by wax.
It is the string in the centre of the candle that burns, but if it were not surrounded by wax the string would burn very quickly. The wax melts slowly and allows the candle to last longer.

Wax causes a candle to burn slowly.

Is iron always hard?

Iron is normally hard and strong. However, when it is heated to a very high temperature, it melts. It turns from a solid into a liquid. Iron has to be heated to a temperature of 1539°C before it melts. Iron is melted so it can be moulded into different shapes.

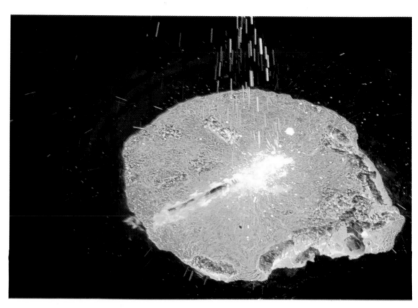

Iron melts when it is heated in a furnace.

How does electricity get to buildings?

Power lines on a pylon.

Electricity is produced at power stations and distributed around the country in cables which are held above the ground on pylons. The electric current passes through sub-stations where it is divided into weaker currents before it enters buildings.

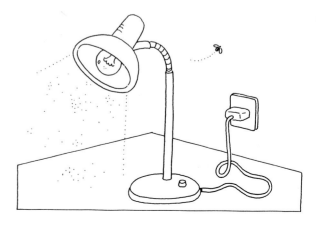

What is a liquid?

A liquid is something that you can pour out of a bottle. It is wet and flowing, and you cannot cut it up. Water is a liquid.

If a liquid is frozen, it turns hard – into a solid. When a liquid is heated beyond a certain temperature, it evaporates and turns into a gas.

Water flowing from a tap.

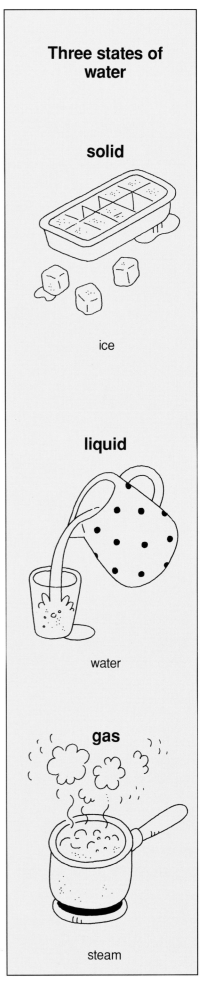

Three states of water

solid

ice

liquid

water

gas

steam

How do bubbles get into fizzy drinks?

Fizzy drinks contain carbon dioxide.

Fizzy drinks do not have bubbles to start with. However, when the gas, carbon dioxide, is added, tiny bubbles rise to the surface of the drink.

Carbon dioxide is added to many drinks to make them fizzy. It is also added to mineral water and beer.

Some springs of mineral water produce water which already has carbon dioxide in it, but these are not as fizzy as drinks that have carbon dioxide added to them.

Why does ice float?

Ice is frozen water. When water freezes, it expands and takes up more room. A chunk of ice is, therefore, lighter than the water it is in, so it floats on the surface. An iceberg floats, although you only see 1/10 of it above the surface.

An iceberg floating in water.

How do hot air balloons stay in the air?

Warm air always rises. A hot air balloon is filled with air which has been heated. This makes it rise above the ground. So long as the air stays hot, the balloon stays up. Every now and then the air in the balloon is reheated.

A hot flame heats the air in a hot air balloon.

Are all days the same length?

A day is made up of a night and a day. There are more daylight hours in summer than in winter, but a day is always 24 hours. This period of time is the time it takes for the Earth to turn round once on its axis.

How does a magnet work?

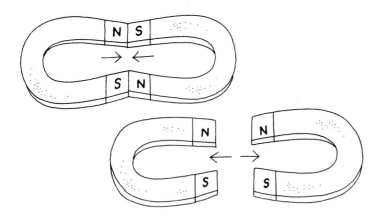

A magnet is a straight or curved piece of metal, such as iron or steel, that attracts other metals. If a magnet is suspended in the air, one end will always point to north and the other to south. If you put two magnets together, the opposite ends, or poles, will attract each other (north and south). When two 'like' poles (north and north) are put together, they repel each other.

Some toys have magnets on them.

a magnet attracts

metals such as:
iron
steel
nickel
cobalt

a magnet does not attract

non-metals such as:
plastic
wood
concrete
metals such as:
aluminium
gold
silver

A clock tells us the time of day.

What is time?

Time always passes. People get older, seasons change, plants die. It is impossible to ignore time and because it is often useful to know a date or an hour, man has divided time into years, months, weeks, days, hours, minutes and seconds. This system is based on the Earth taking 365¼ days to make one complete revolution around the Sun.

Where does heat come from?

Almost all heat comes from the Sun, even the heat which comes from cookers and radiators. This is because coal, oil and gas all come from the compressed remains of plants that lived under the Earth's Sun millions of years ago.

It is pleasant to sit in the Sun's warmth.

Which objects are levers?

Many of the objects that we use every day are levers. For example, scissors, nutcrackers, bottle openers and wheelbarrows.
A wheelbarrow has its support, or fulcrum, at the wheel so that when you lift up the

These bridges are raised by levers.

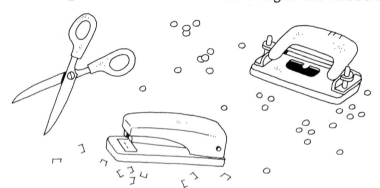

handles, the weight rests on the wheel and not on your arms.
This enables you to move a heavy weight around.

Lightning is a form of electricity.

What is electricity?

An atom is the smallest part of a chemical element. Each atom is surrounded by electrons. When the electrons are all moving together in the same direction, a current of energy is created called electricity. Lightning is a huge spark of static electricity between the clouds and the ground.

natural light

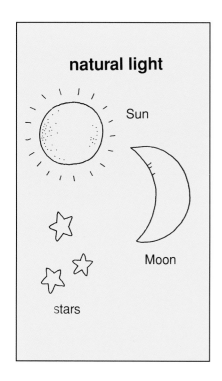

Sun

Moon

stars

artificial light

matches

torch

street light

desk lamp

bicycle light

What is light?

The Sun gives off rays of light. Whatever part of the Earth is facing the Sun receives these rays of light. The part of the Earth that is not facing the Sun is in darkness. If the Sun's light did not reach the Earth we would be in darkness all the time. However, man has invented ways of producing light by using gas or electricity. When the Sun sets, we turn on appliances that produce artificial light.

Electric lights are used when the Sun has set.

How are sounds recorded?

Sound can be recorded on a cassette.

A cassette recorder has a magnetic band which is made up of tiny metallic particles. During a recording, sound is converted into an electric current. The current causes the particles of metal to arrange themselves in certain patterns. The sound that is heard depends on the patterns.

What happens when water boils?

Water is made up of molecules. When water is heated, the molecules move about very quickly and at 100°C they leave the water as steam. Water bubbles when it boils because oxygen is leaving it.

Steam from a boiling kettle.

What are fireworks made of?

Fireworks are made of cardboard tubes containing gunpowder and small amounts of other substances that produce colour.
In this country we let off fireworks on Bonfire Night to celebrate the fact that on the 5th of November, 1605, Guy Fawkes was stopped from setting light to barrels of gunpowder and blowing up the Houses of Parliament.

Fireworks light up the sky.

What is meant by 'mechanics'?

Mechanics is a scientific subject that deals with motion and the effects of forces on objects. Mechanics come into our lives every day. Just lifting a chair and moving it from one place to another involves mechanics.

Does air weigh anything?

The air around us does not weigh very much, in fact it is difficult to believe that it weighs anything at all. In areas of lowland air weighs about 1.2 grams.

Can you travel into the future?

Flying to a different country and time zone.

No, it is impossible to travel into the future or back to the past. However, because of the different time zones around the world, it is possible to leave London by aeroplane at 7 pm and arrive in New York at 5 pm the same day – even though the flight took five hours. This is because the world is divided into different time zones. The time zones mean that countries to the west of Britain are 1-12 hours behind, and to the east of Britain they are 1-12 hours ahead.

Can water split rocks?

Ice can split a rock.

Even if there is only a tiny crack in a rock, water will get in. When the water freezes and expands it forces the crack to get wider. Eventually the rock splits along the crack.

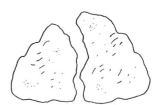

Which are the primary colours?

The three main (primary) colours of light are red, blue and green. When these colours are mixed together, they produce white light. The primary colours of paint are red, blue and yellow. These colours are mixed to produce other colours.

There are many different shades of colour.

An electric power station.

How is electricity produced?

Currents of electricity are produced by generators.
A generator has a big engine, or turbine, that turns mechanical energy into electricity. The engine is usually powered by steam or water.
Nowadays, however, nuclear power stations produce heat that is used to power the generators.

How does water put out a fire?

Flames of fire need oxygen in order to burn. If water is thrown on a fire, it prevents oxygen from reaching the burning object and the fire

Flames of fire need oxygen to burn.

goes out. The door of a burning room should be closed so that the fire is starved of oxygen. Throwing water on a burning object also helps to cool it down.

What are stalactites and stalagmites?

Rock is a very hard substance. However, if it contains limestone (calcium carbonate), rain-water eats away at this softer substance until, after thousands of years, a cave forms.
The tiny particles of limestone which fall with the rainwater to the floor of the cave, form columns called stalagmites.
The drips that remain on the roof of the cave form icicle-shaped stalactites. Stalactites and stalagmites take thousands of years to form.

Stalactites and stalagmites in an underground cave.

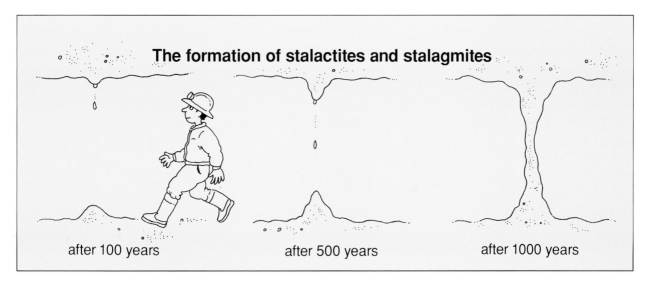

The formation of stalactites and stalagmites

after 100 years   after 500 years   after 1000 years

What is a transformer?

It is dangerous to use an electric current from a socket if the power (voltage) is too strong.
A transformer changes a strong current into a weaker one.

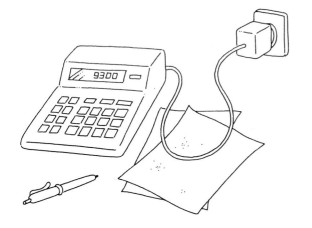

An electric train and a transformer.

Transformers are sometimes used in the home or office for electrical appliances.

What is a conductor?

Wires in the cord conduct electricity to the iron.

A conductor is a material that lets a current of electricity pass along it.
Metals are usually good conductors. Copper wire is often used to conduct electricity. It is used on high buildings to conduct lightning to the ground.
Materials that do not conduct electricity are called insulators.

How do aeroplanes fly?

An aeroplane is thrust forward by its engines, but this alone does not make it airborn. This is caused by the shape of its wings. The upper side of each

Aeroplanes flying in formation.

wing curves outwards so air moves faster over the top than the bottom and causes an uplift.

What happens when water freezes?

Water freezes at a temperature of 0°C (32°F). When water freezes, it becomes hard and is called ice. Freezing water expands and that is why ice cubes are made in plastic containers as they do not break when ice forms.

Why do people wear white in summer?

White reflects light and heat. This is why most summer clothes are white. People who live in hot countries often wear long white gowns and paint their houses white. Black, on the other hand,

White clothes keep you cool in summer.

absorbs light and heat.

If you touch the roof of a black car and a white car on a hot, sunny day, you will soon notice the difference! The roof of the black car will feel much hotter. Wearing black clothes in summer makes you feel hot.

Why is lightning dangerous?

It is often the sound of thunder that is frightening to children and adults. However, thunder is completely harmless. It is just a noise. Lightning, on the other hand, is a bolt of electricity, which if it strikes a tree, may set fire to it.

How is time measured?

Without an idea of time, it would be difficult to arrange to meet people. So, a long time ago, man invented ways of measuring time, such as sundials and sand-filled timers. However, these were not accurate and eventually clocks and watches were invented.

An old-fashioned watch.

Can you see and feel air?

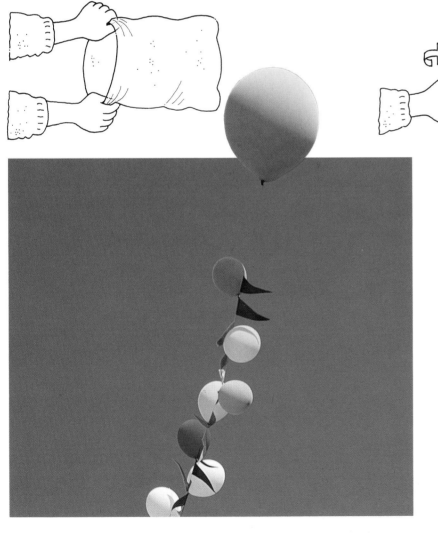

If you run, you can feel the air against your face. You can also feel the air when the wind blows. If you pull an open plastic bag, through the air and then close it tightly, you can feel the air in the bag. You cannot see air – it is an invisible gas.

You cannot see air.

Why do all objects fall to Earth?

Any large object attracts other objects towards it. The Earth also attracts objects towards it – this is called gravity. If you drop something, it is pulled down towards the Earth by gravity.

A parachute slows the fall.

How is wastewater purified?

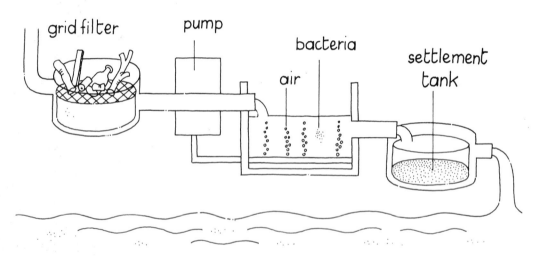

grid filter — pump — air — bacteria — settlement tank

Water is aerated at a water treatment works.

Wastewater is filtered through grids before it passes into a tank where bits of grit fall to the bottom. Next, the water is whipped to a froth in an aeration tank. This kills any bacteria. The water passes into another tank before it goes to the river.

Equipment in a chemistry laboratory

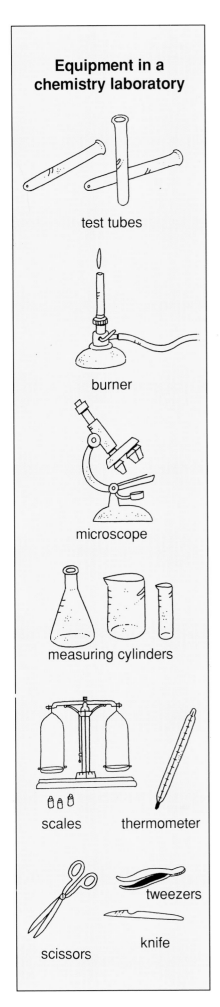

test tubes

burner

microscope

measuring cylinders

scales thermometer

tweezers

scissors knife

What is chemistry?

Chemists analyse different substances.

Chemistry is the study of the make-up of substances. Scientists look closely at the elements, atoms and molecules of a substance. They also observe how these work and their reaction with each other. Scientists use their discoveries to make such useful materials as plastic and nylon.

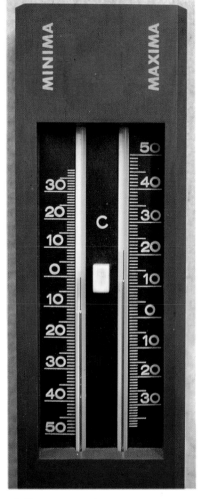

A thermometer.

How is heat measured?

Heat can be measured by going outside and standing in the garden. You will decide whether the temperature is hot or cold. You may also test the water of a bath to see if it is too hot. However, sometimes we need to know exactly how hot or cold things are. Then we use a thermometer.

A thermometer measures heat in degrees in Centigrade or Fahrenheit. Scientists use special thermometers to measure extremely cold and hot temperatures.

The boiling points of . . .

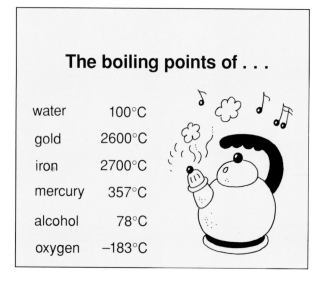

water	100°C
gold	2600°C
iron	2700°C
mercury	357°C
alcohol	78°C
oxygen	−183°C

The freezing points of . . .

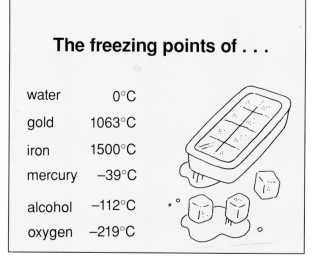

water	0°C
gold	1063°C
iron	1500°C
mercury	−39°C
alcohol	−112°C
oxygen	−219°C

How many colours are there in a rainbow?

A rainbow is an arc of coloured light that usually appears after a shower on a sunny day.

Sunlight is usually colourless, but when it passes through drops of water it is split into red, orange, yellow, green, blue, indigo and violet.

A rainbow has seven colours.

What are magnets used for?

The needle of a compass is a magnet.

Magnets can be found in many everyday objects. Cassettes, fridge doors, telephones all use magnets. The needle of a compass is a magnet and one end (pole) of the needle will always point to the north. The Earth is an enormous magnet with a North and South Pole.

How fast does light travel?

Rays of light from the Sun.

The Sun sends out light in all directions. Light travels in short waves which always move in straight lines.

Waves of light from the Sun take eight minutes to pass through space and reach Earth. Light from the Moon takes less than a second because the Moon is much closer.

Light travels at a speed equivalent to 186,000 miles per second. Nothing on Earth can move this fast.

Is it possible to compress liquid?

Water is a liquid and, unlike gases, liquids cannot be compressed.

For example, if you fill a bottle full to the brim with water and try to push a cork in, you will find that it is impossible to do.

Why do things move and stop?

Nothing will move unless there is a force making it do so. A bicycle, for example, will not move unless you turn the pedals.

You cannot move your limbs unless you contract and relax certain muscles.

The same is true of stopping. For a moving object to stop, there has to be a force making it do so – even if it is only the resistance of air.

A bicycle chain links the pedals to a wheel.

What is a laser?

A powerful laser beam.

A laser is a machine that produces a narrow beam of light. However, the light is no ordinary light. It is very powerful. The beam is capable of cutting through metal. It is used in surgery, telecommunications and dental work.

Why is soap used to clean dirt away?

Washing up detergent is a type of soap.

If you get oil and dirt on your hands, water alone will not clean it away. The water simply rolls off grease. However, if you use soap, it will penetrate the grease and break it up into tiny particles that can be rinsed away. Soaps are made from alkalis, such as caustic soda and caustic potash.

How does a battery work?

A battery contains cells that make electricity.

A battery contains a rod which is surrounded by salt, and contained inside a zinc casing.

When the battery is used, two conductors are connected and the zinc and salt create an electric current.

When either the salt or the zinc is used up, the battery is flat.

contact point

salt

rod

zinc

Index

Sources of photographs

Alcatel Bell: 4, 6, 25 t; British Embassy: 31 b; Electrabel: 20 t; Greenpeace: 10 b; Grohe: 9; Hendrikx, I.: 2, 3 b, 5, 7, 8, 10 t, 11, 12, 13 t, 15, 16 b, 17, 18, 19 b, 20 b, 21, 22 b, 23, 24, 25 b, 26, 27, 28, 29 b, 31 t, 32; Nagels, I.: 3t, 14 t, 22 t, 29 t, 30; Nasa: 13 b; NOOA: 19 t; Sony: 16 t.